TEETERING THE LINE:

An Adult Coloring Book

by Dan Drossman

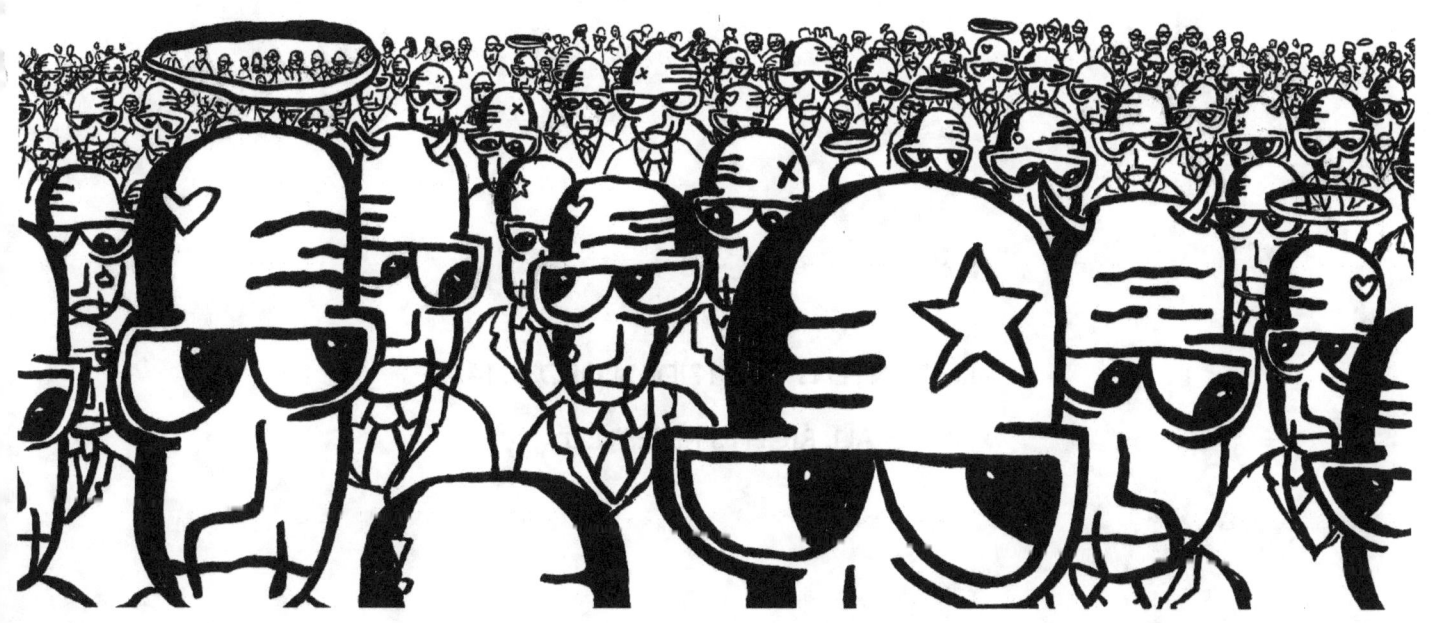

Thank you for supporting my first
Adult Coloring Book! I would love to hear
what you have to say about it, so please write
a review on my Amazon page.

What I am most excited about is seeing how
you have re-colored the work, so please share
them on my Facebook Page @teeteringtheline.

Keep on coloring!

An Introduction

Teetering The Line: An Adult Coloring Book—a collection of original artworks by contemporary artist, street artist, cartoonist, and illustrator, Dan Drossman—is not the oversized art designed for a glance or gaze at the side of a building or gallery wall. These images are far more intimate. They demand more attention, creativity, and introspection—by you.

"When I started these drawings, my life seemed entirely monochromatic." Instead of trying to run from the drabness, Drossman let it flow over him and into his materials, a catharsis that impelled the creation of one drawing per day for one year, with no intention of producing a coloring book. "The more I colored the drawings, the more I emerged from a bland fog into a world of color, and started to enjoy life again."

The 22 drawings in *Teetering The Line* saw Drossman moving in and out of cathartic bursts of emotional graffiti that finally delivered him to a space far from the routines of today's over-connected world, with its internet-frenetic culture of distraction and quick agenda. The space held no cell-phones, television, technology, social media, or updating "statuses." It was a space of sheer, focused creativity. While in it, the idea struck that a coloring book might provide the perfect vessel for people to re- colorize their own worlds by coloring within his designated lines and contours. And who's not nostalgic for the coloring books of their youth?

"As a kid, I would pull my green crayon bucket from under my parents bed, color in my books, and teleport to a calmer world of line and color." It was that timelessness, plus the smell of fresh crayons and the thrilling smears of colored wax across paper, which inspired Drossman to again seek the present. "I wanted to share that strong, early feeling with others in their own therapeutic process by helping reflect back the emotional palette they might discover by adding their own colors to my drawings."

The black and white drawings in this book once gleamed with color, but the artist has extracted it so others can channel their own interpretations in their return of color —not to pretty pictures of common tropes, but to a finer art exploring our relations to our world, our selves, and the reasons we should deploy color in the first place. Drossman's art, even without color, is bold, funny, intricate, mysterious, disturbed, and fantastic. Eternal rainclouds explode into spectrums, grand shapes shatter into fragments, or strange worlds resolve amid backdrops of 80s-era video games—all the while observed by figures, sharp and mechanized, soft and angelic, but always wary.

"Imagination colors the world. It's important to respire the impulse sparked by the color. Having an outline can provide the 'permission' to experience vibrancies close at hand. The mundane 'out there' can overwhelm. I'd had enough, and this is my reaction." In this wonderfully unique and innovative adult coloring book, Drossman encourages you to react by recoloring your own world with markers, colored pencils, pens, and your imagination. Throw your color around Drossman's spaces, experience color, and take it as your own, because *Teetering The Line: An Adult Coloring Book* is that creative color meditation inviting you to teeter your own line.

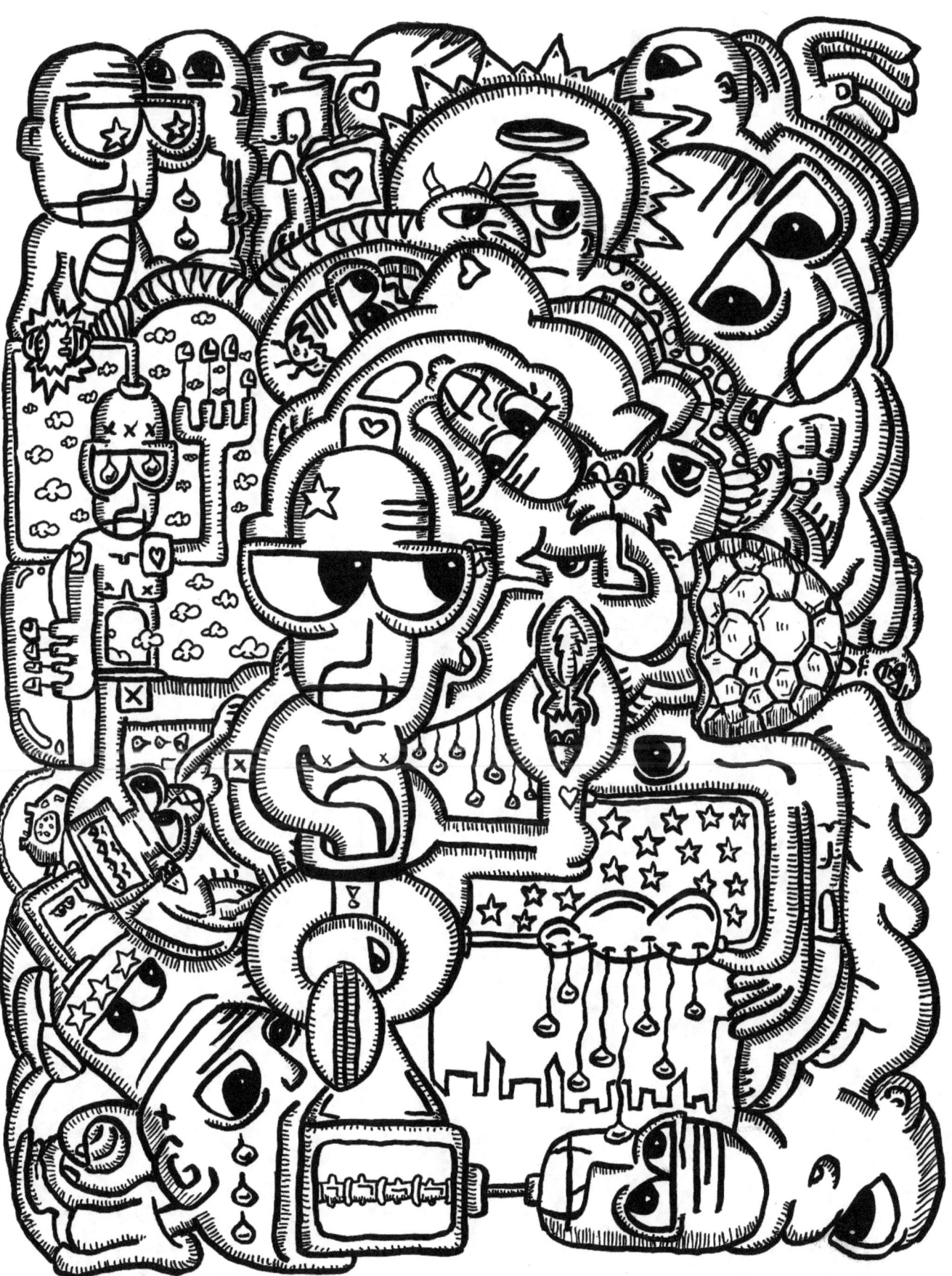

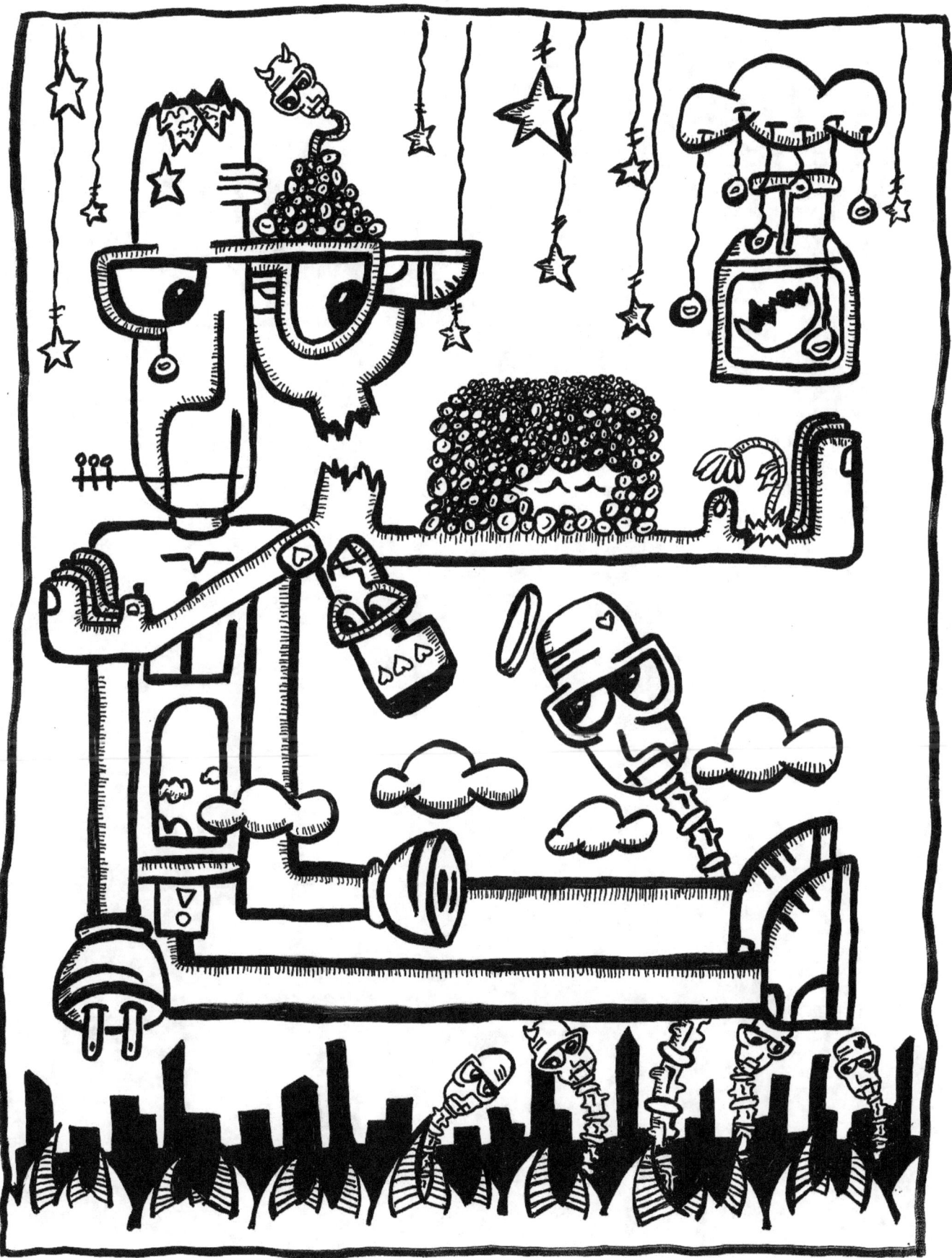

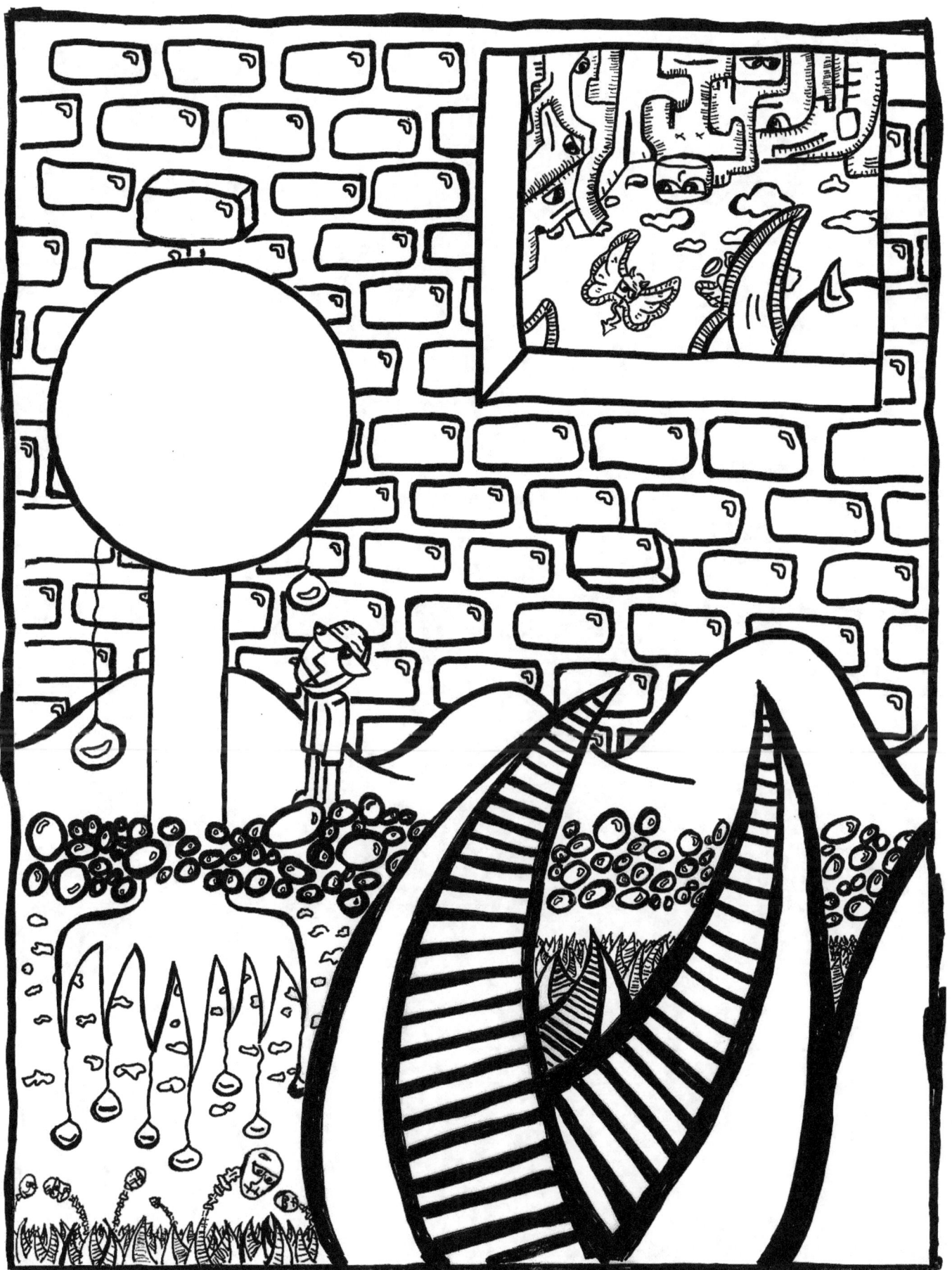

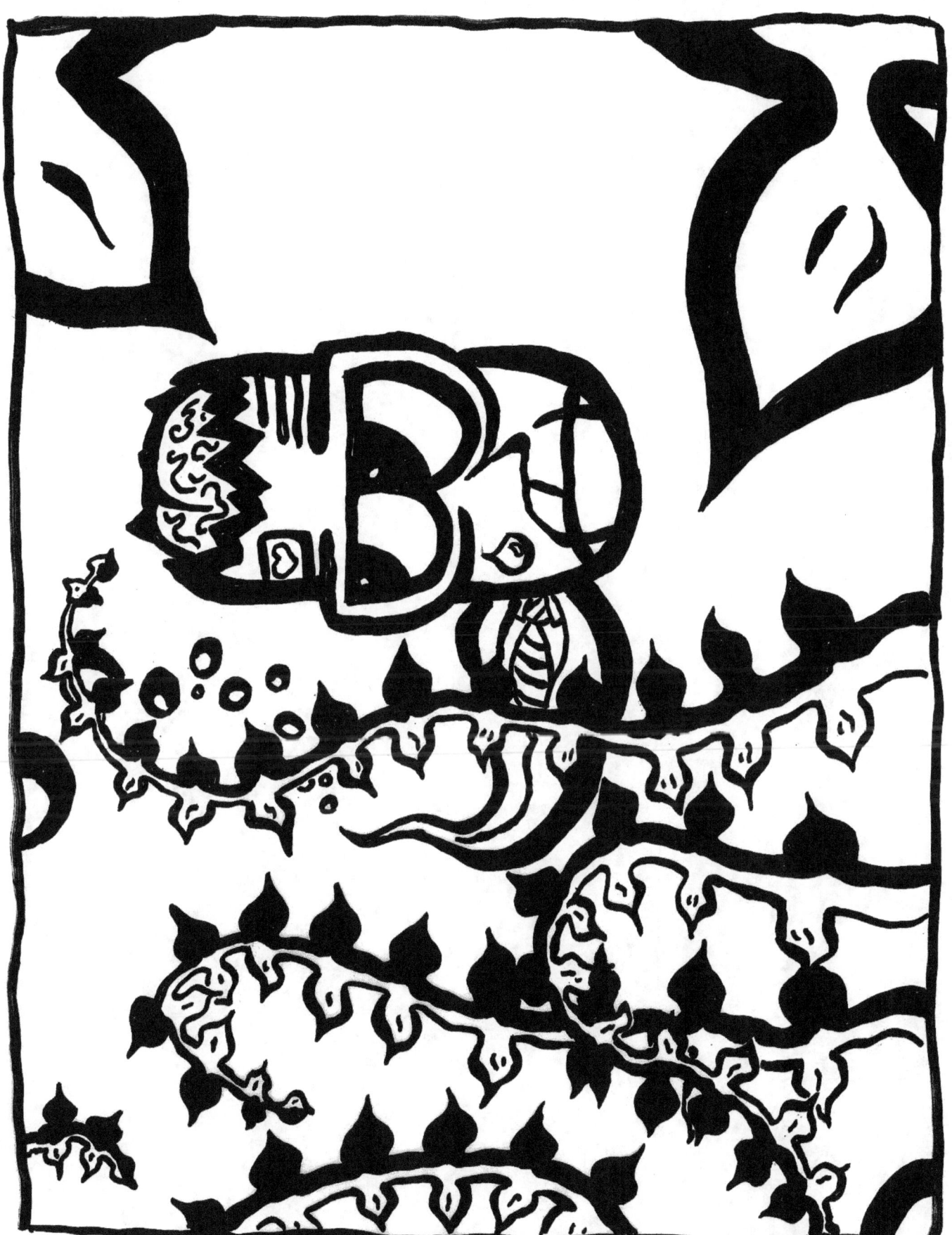

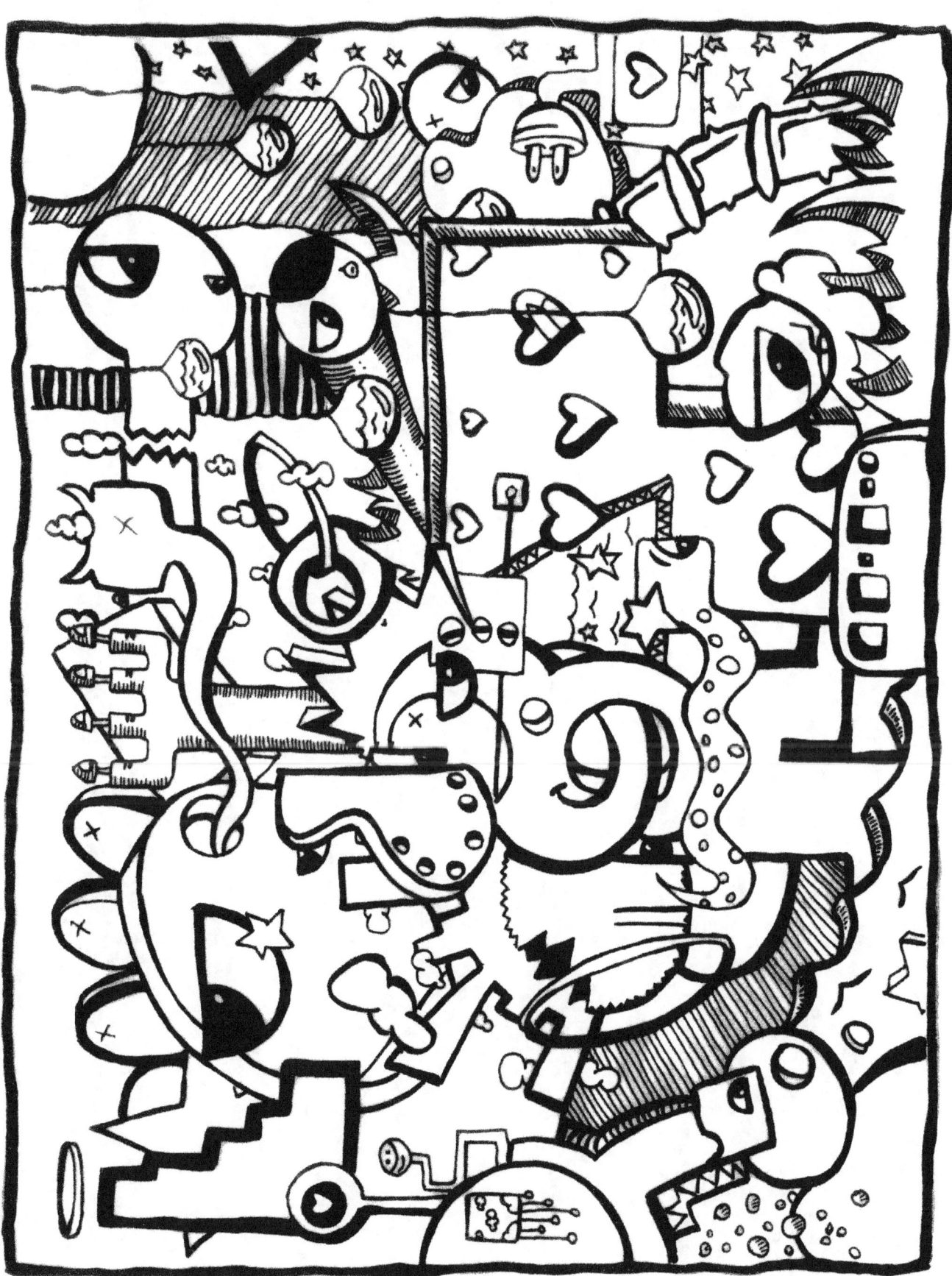

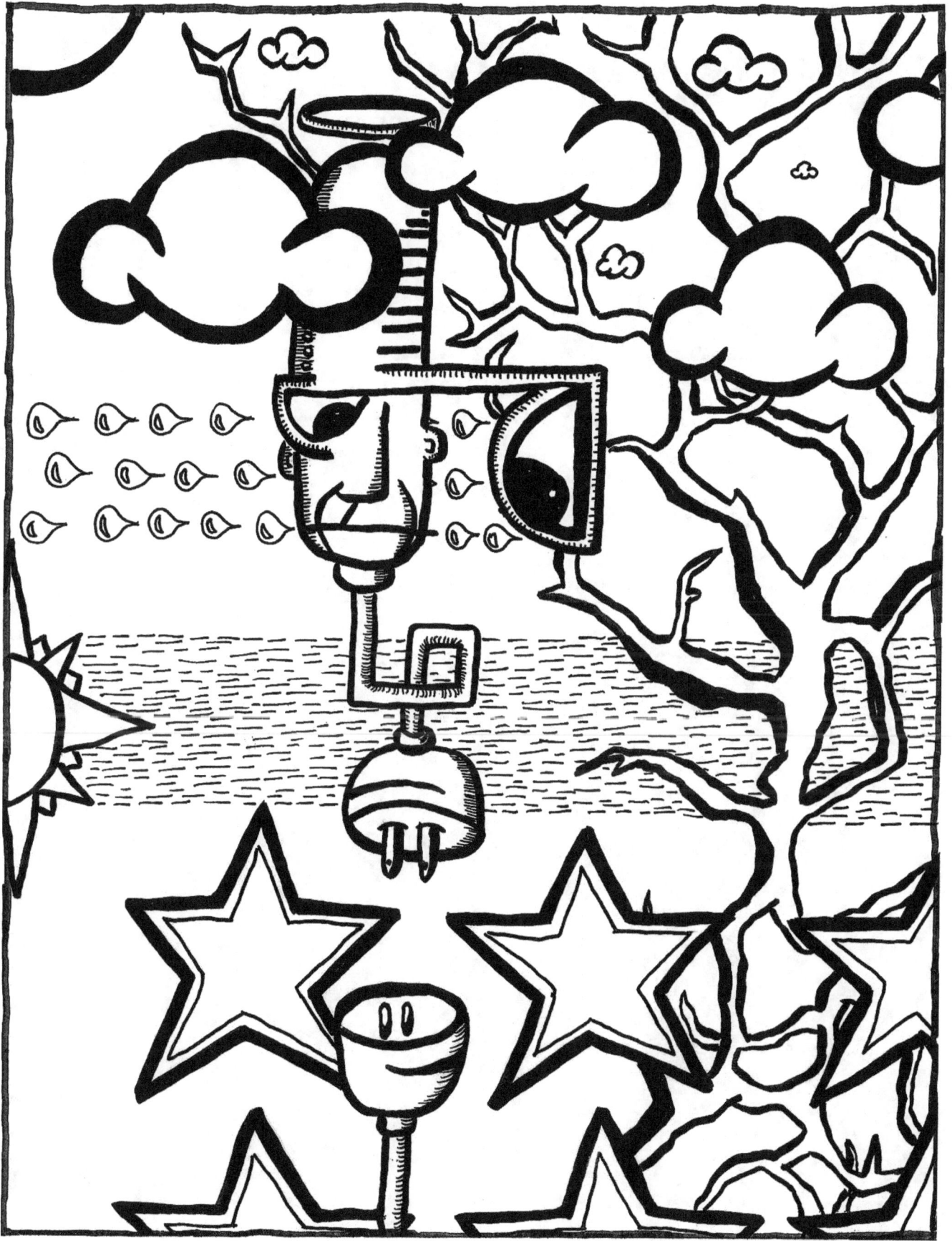

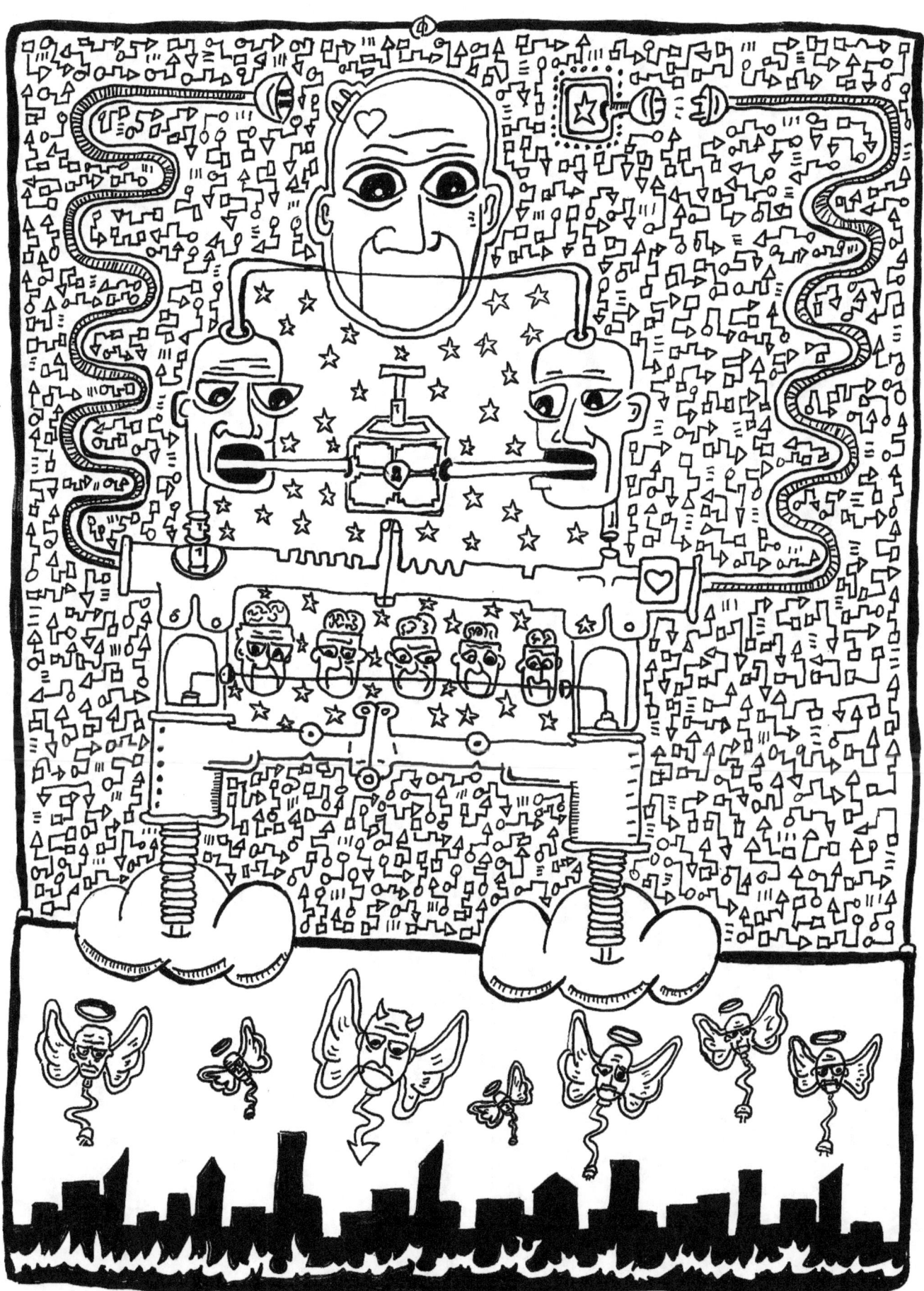

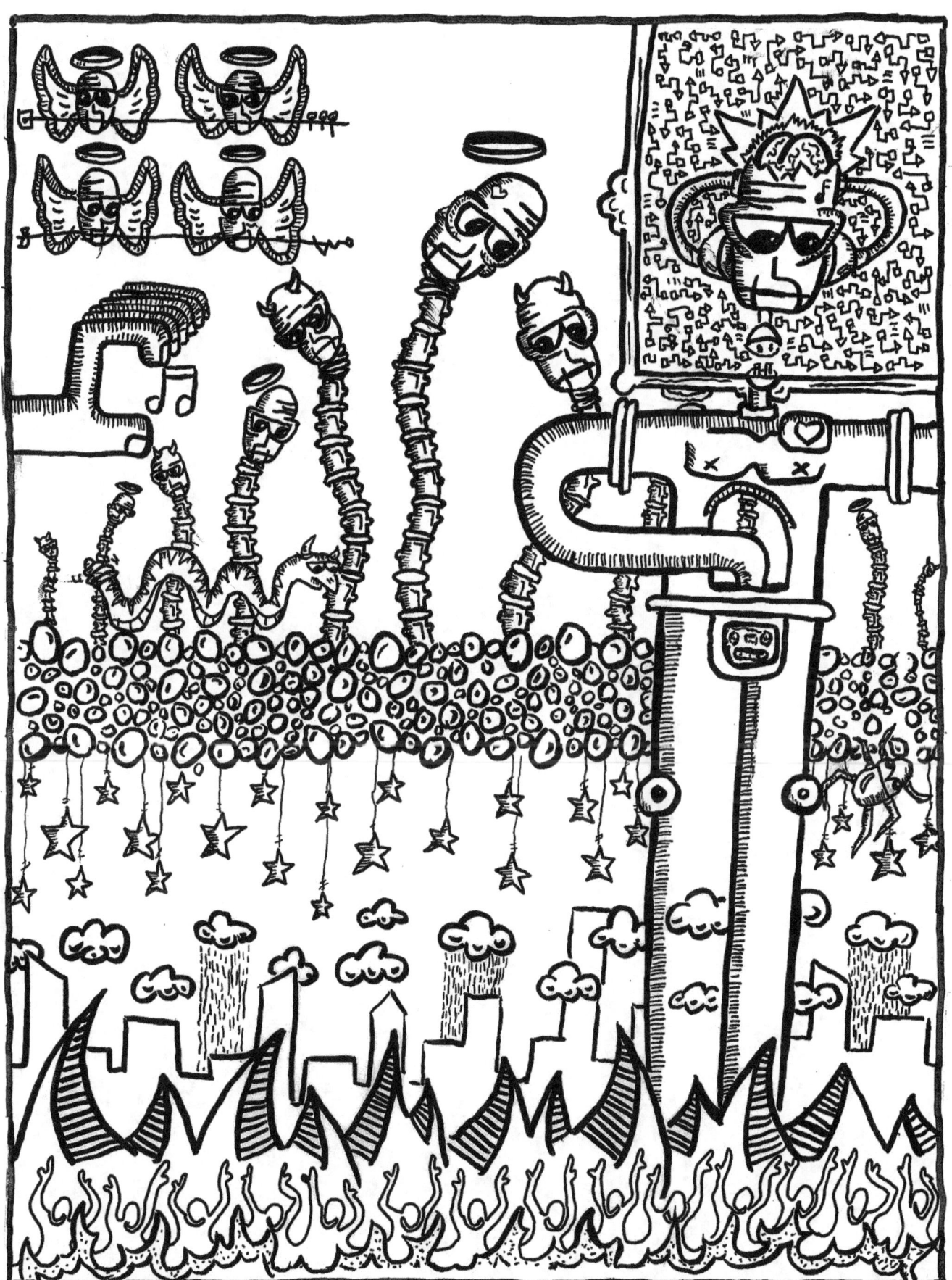

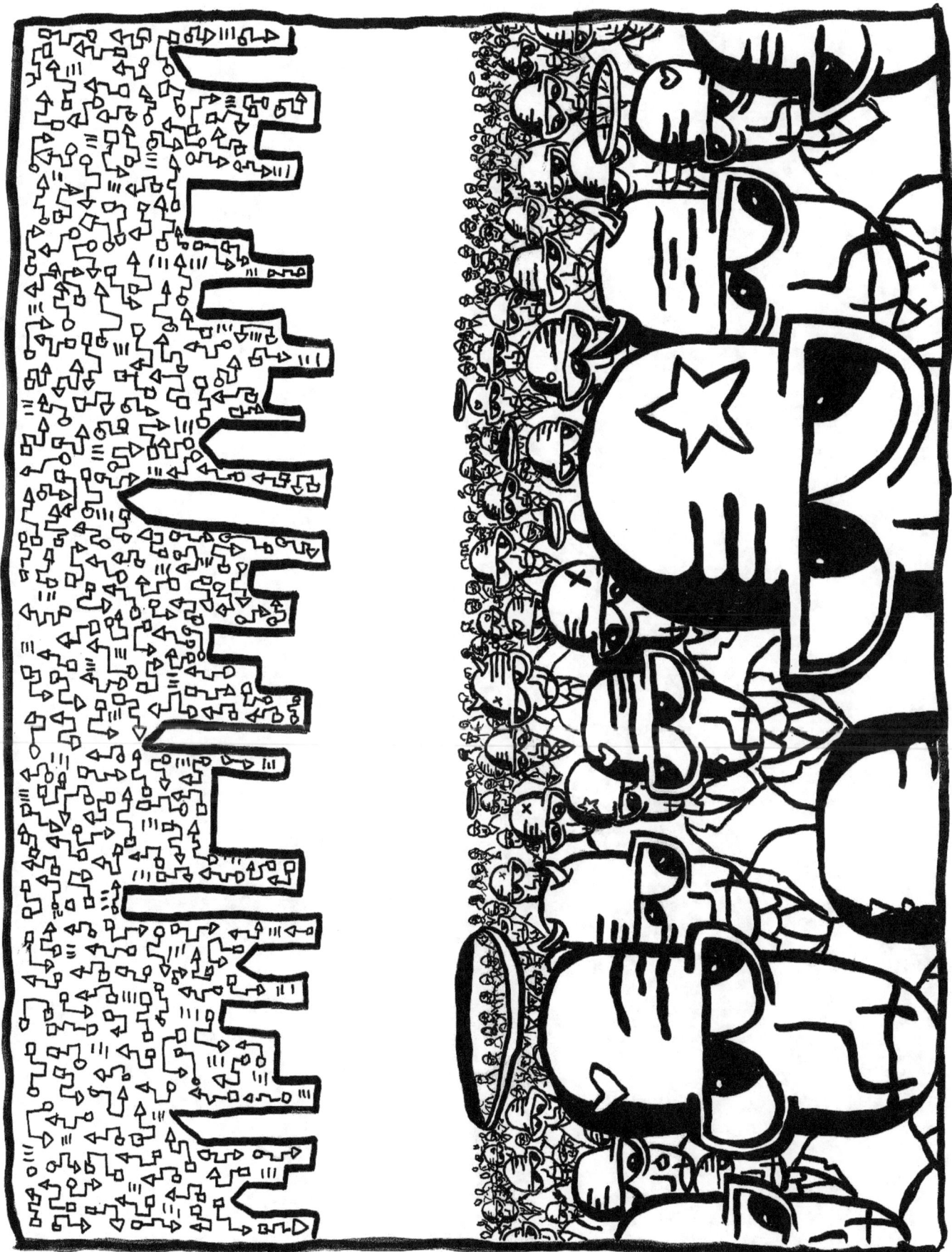

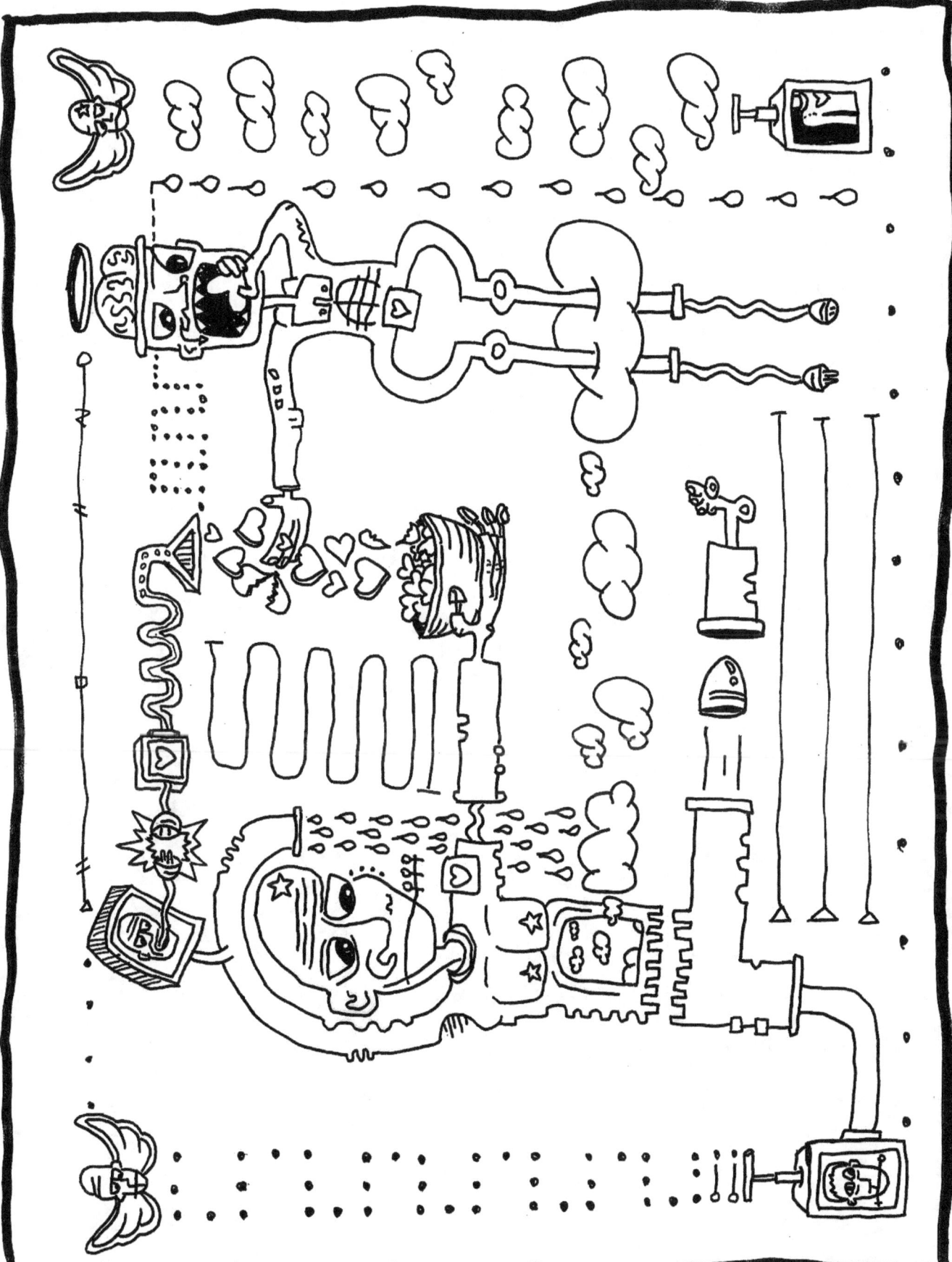

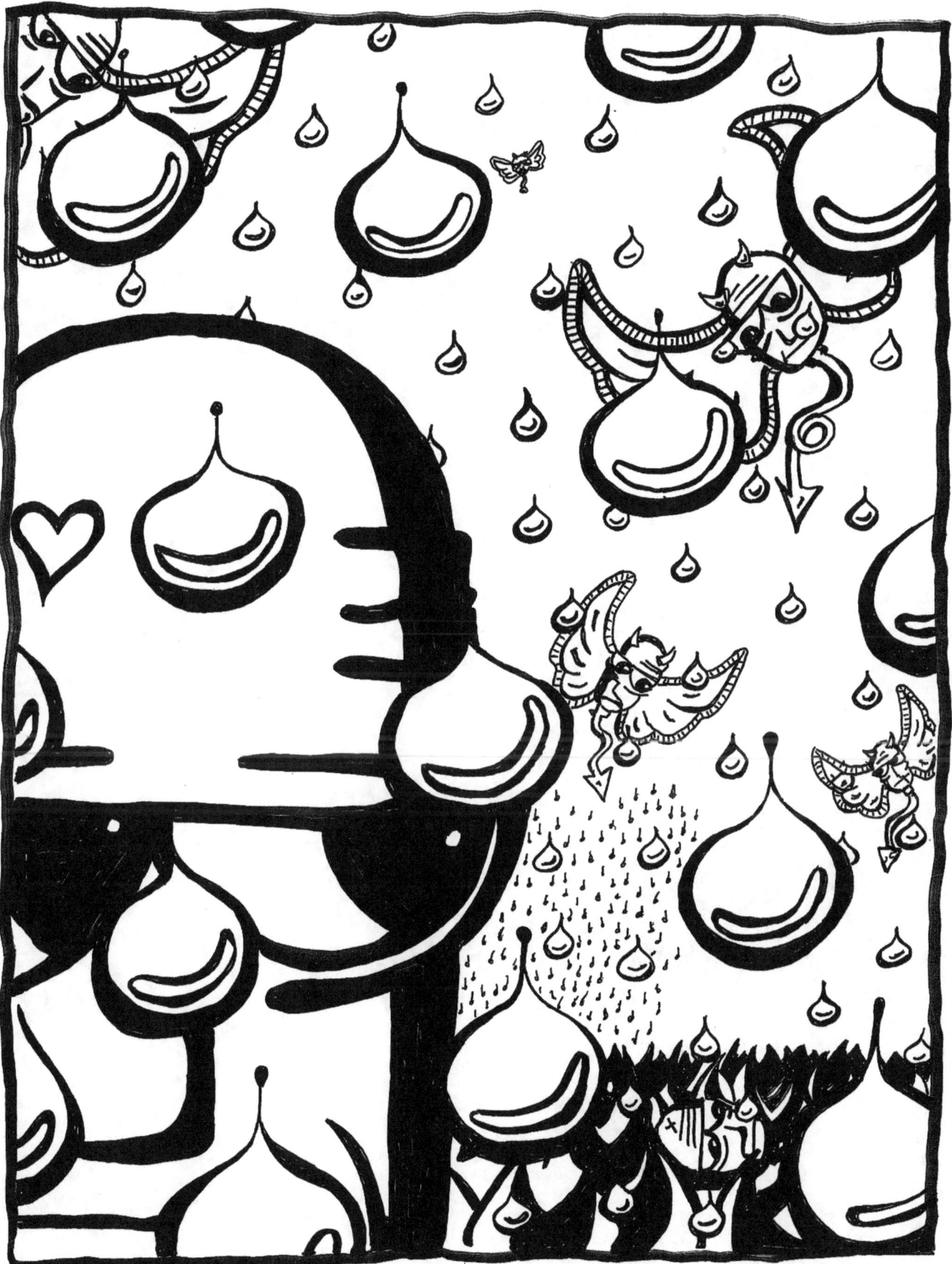

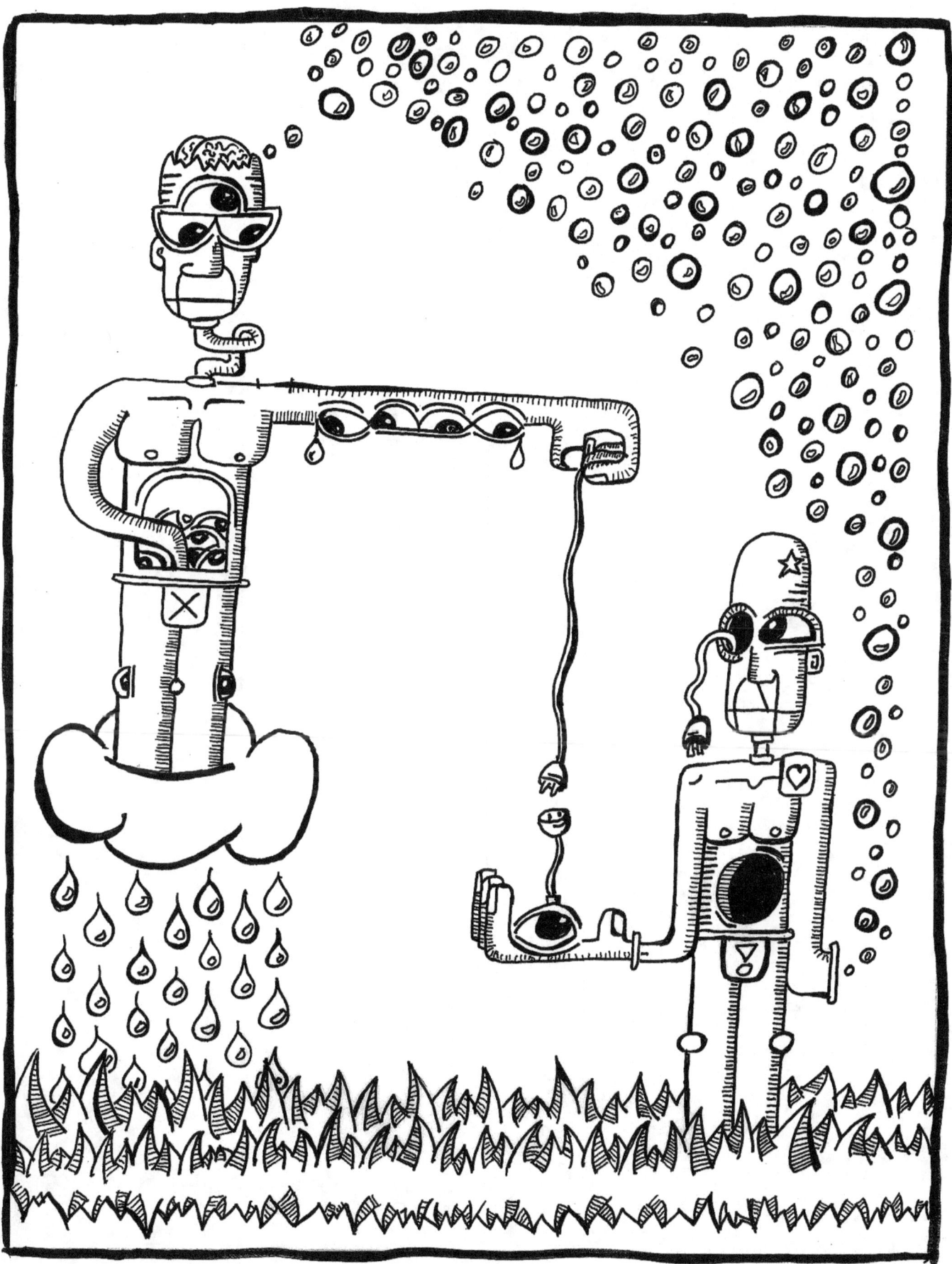

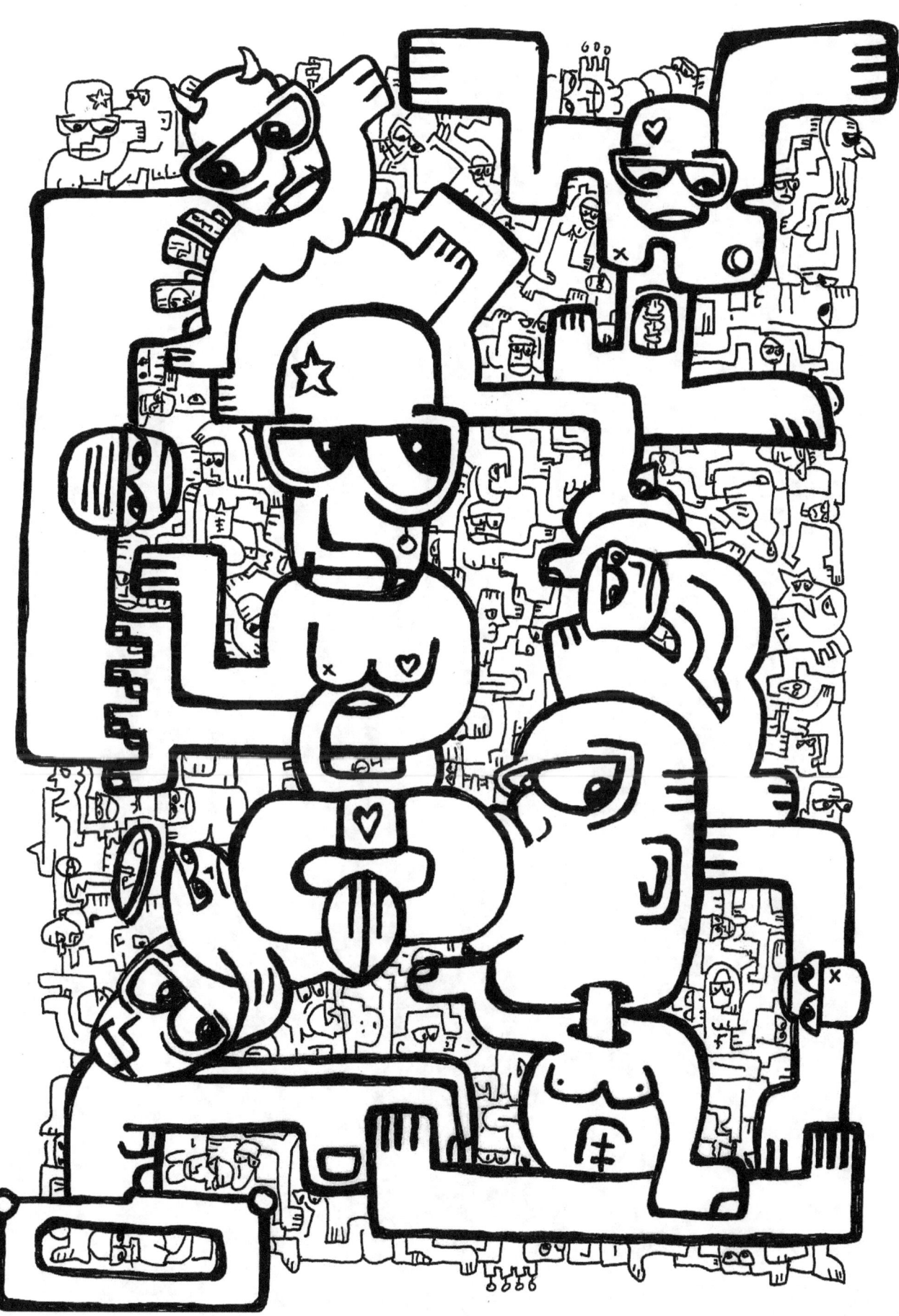

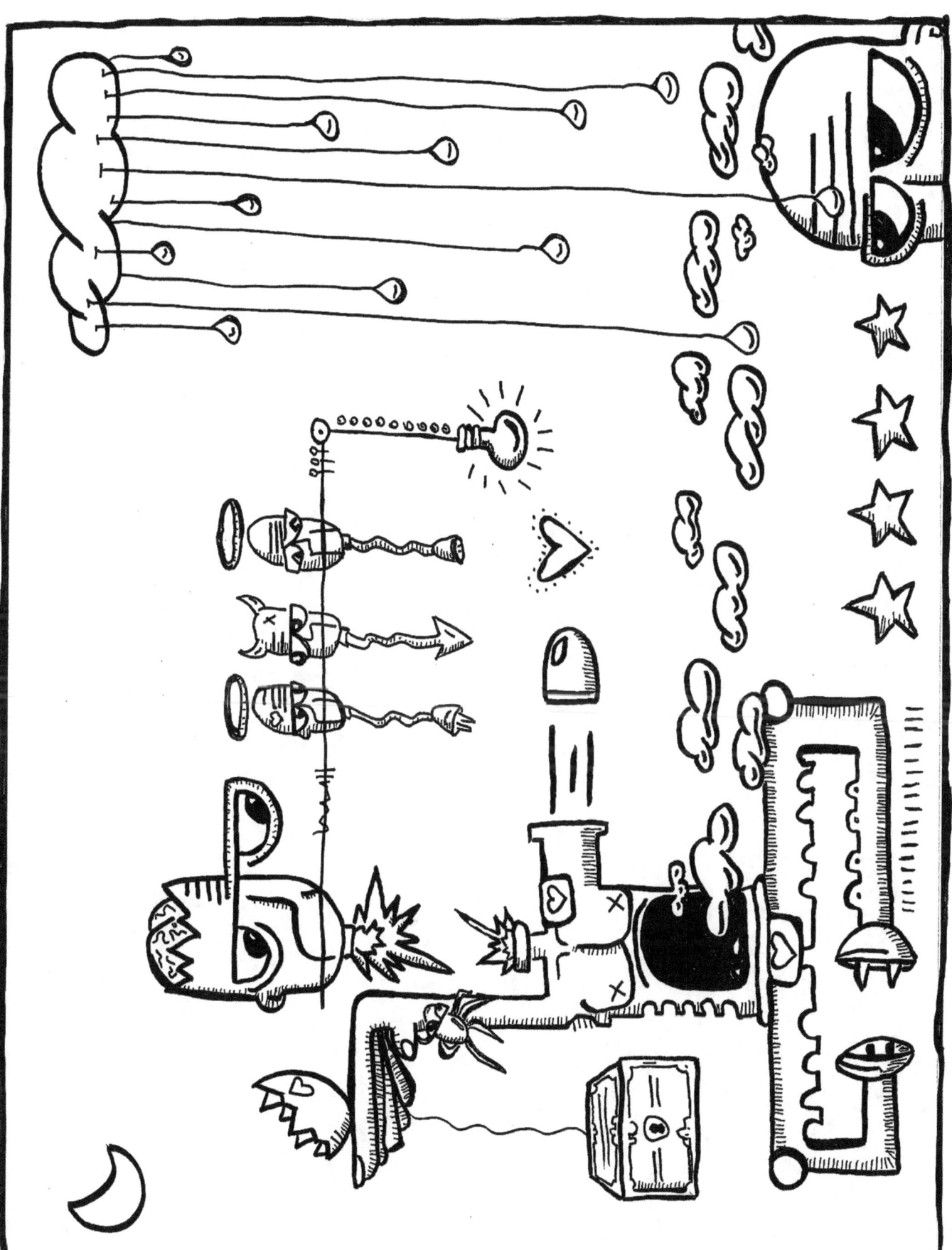

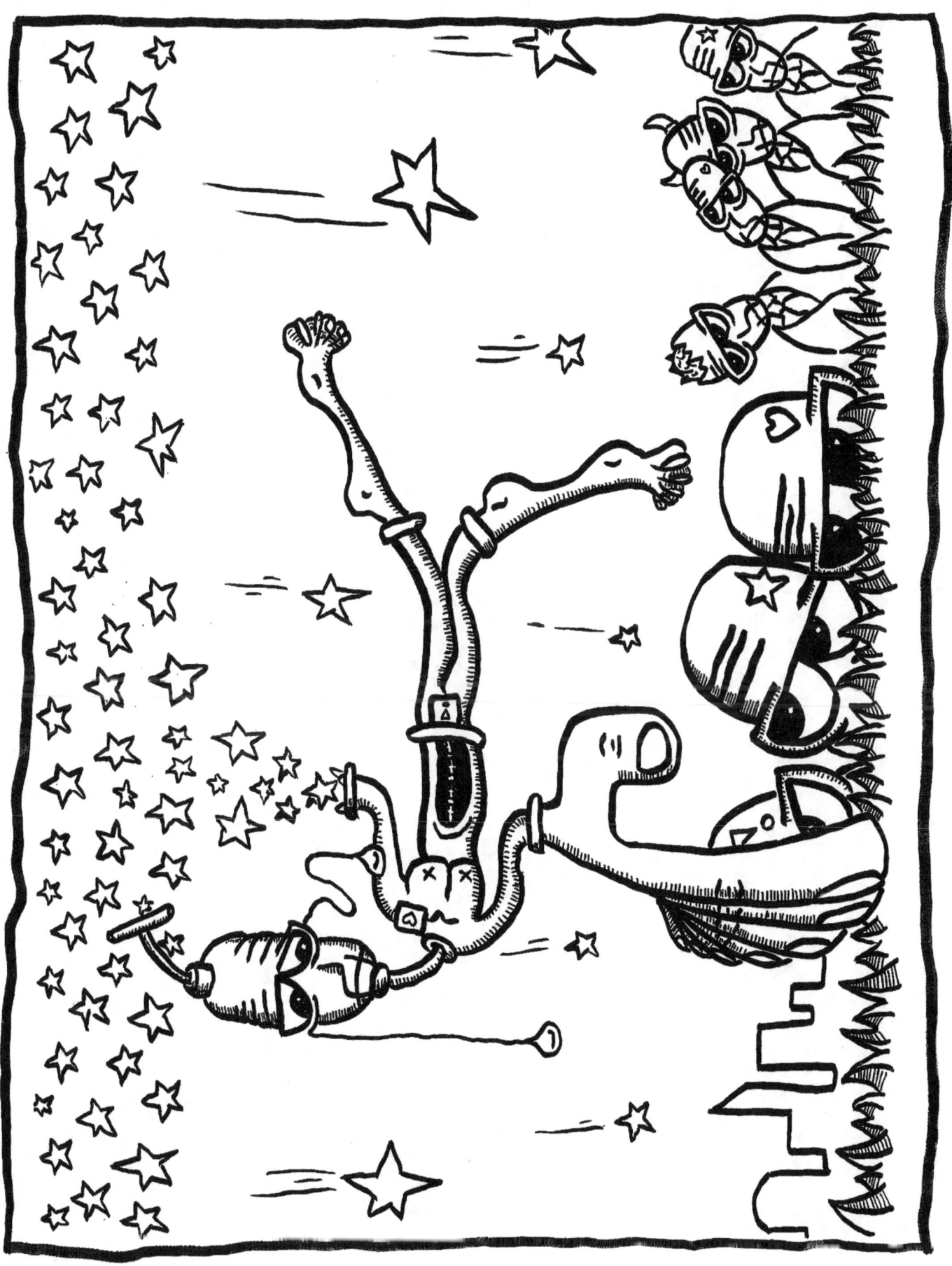

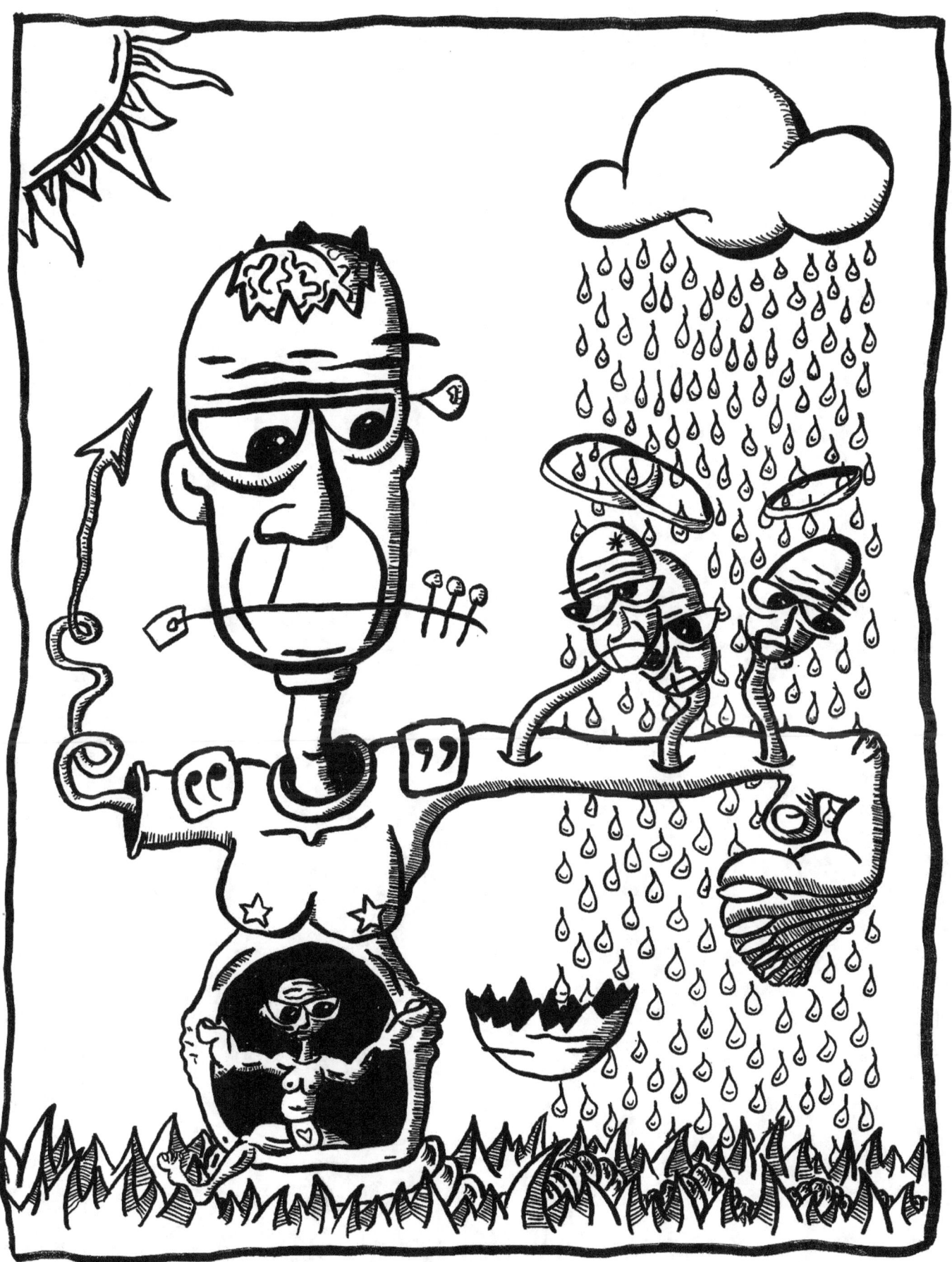

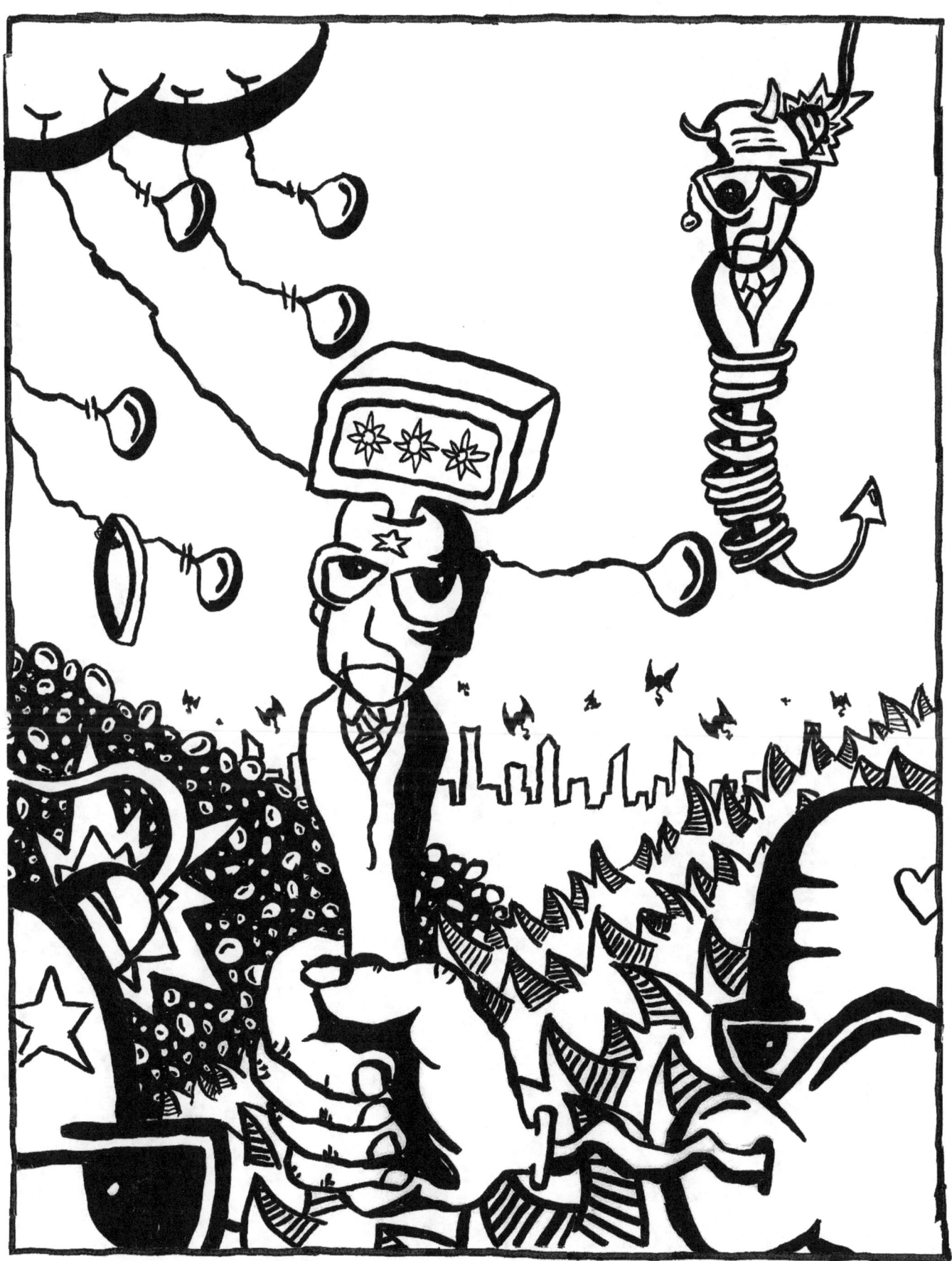

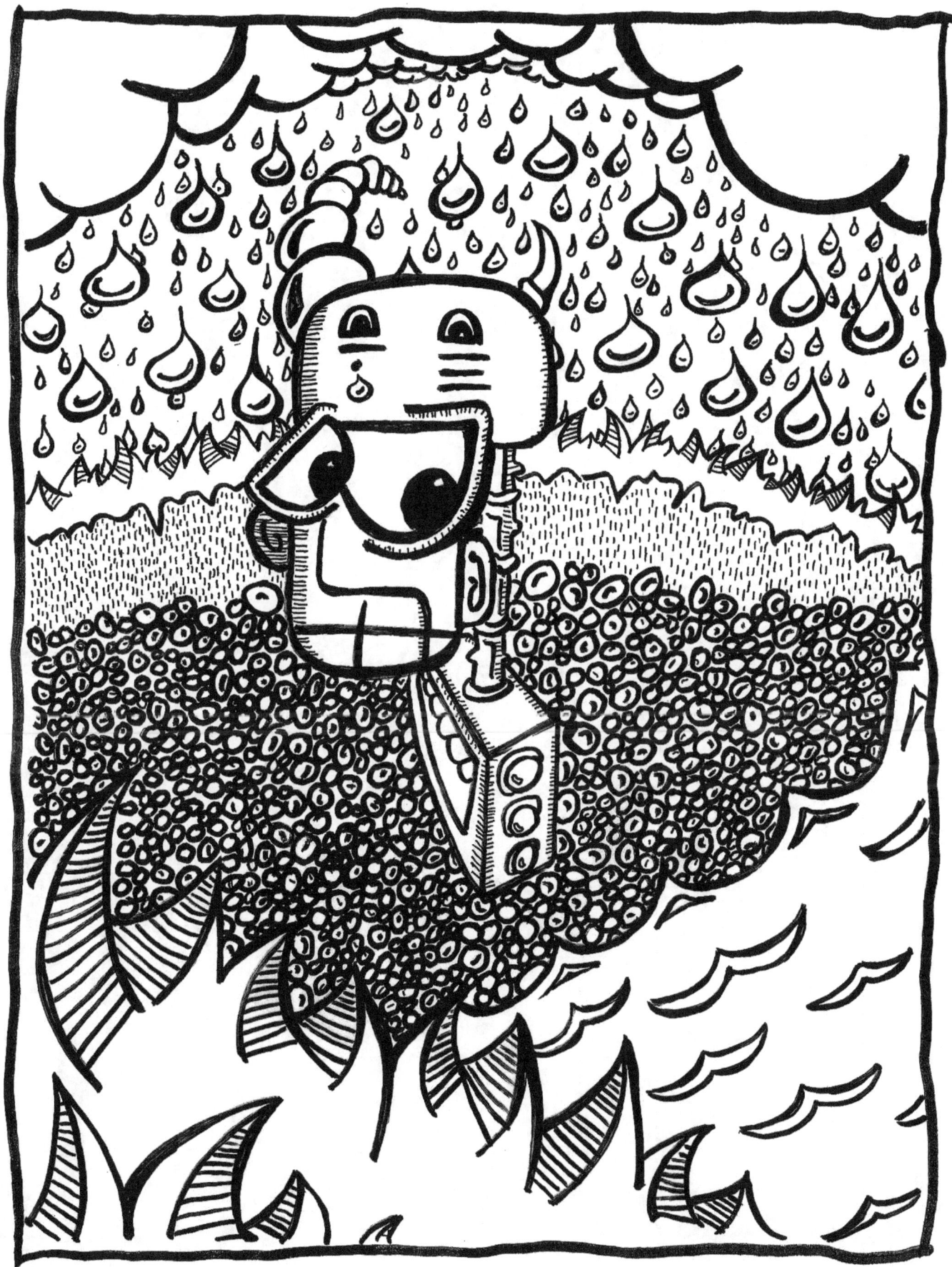

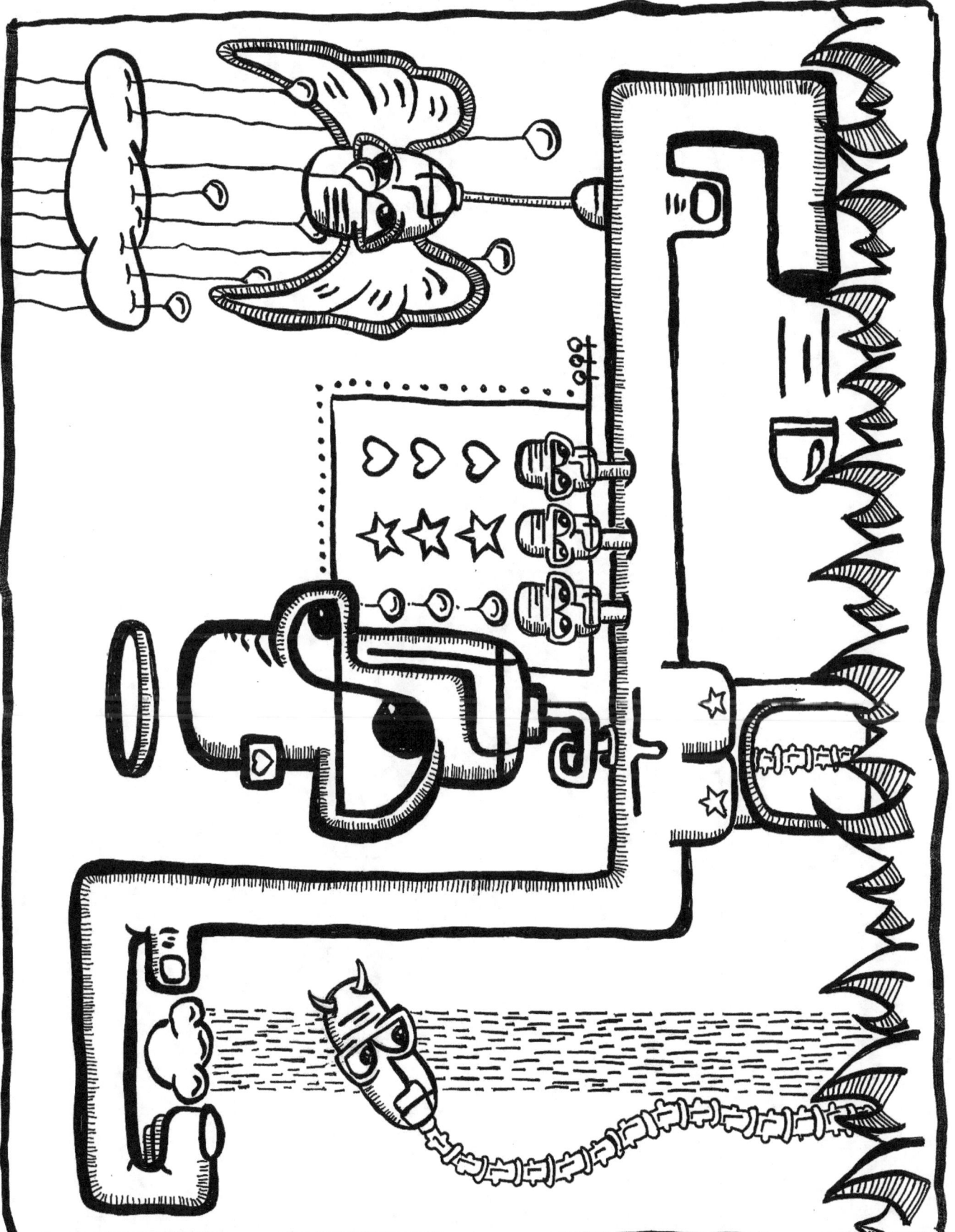

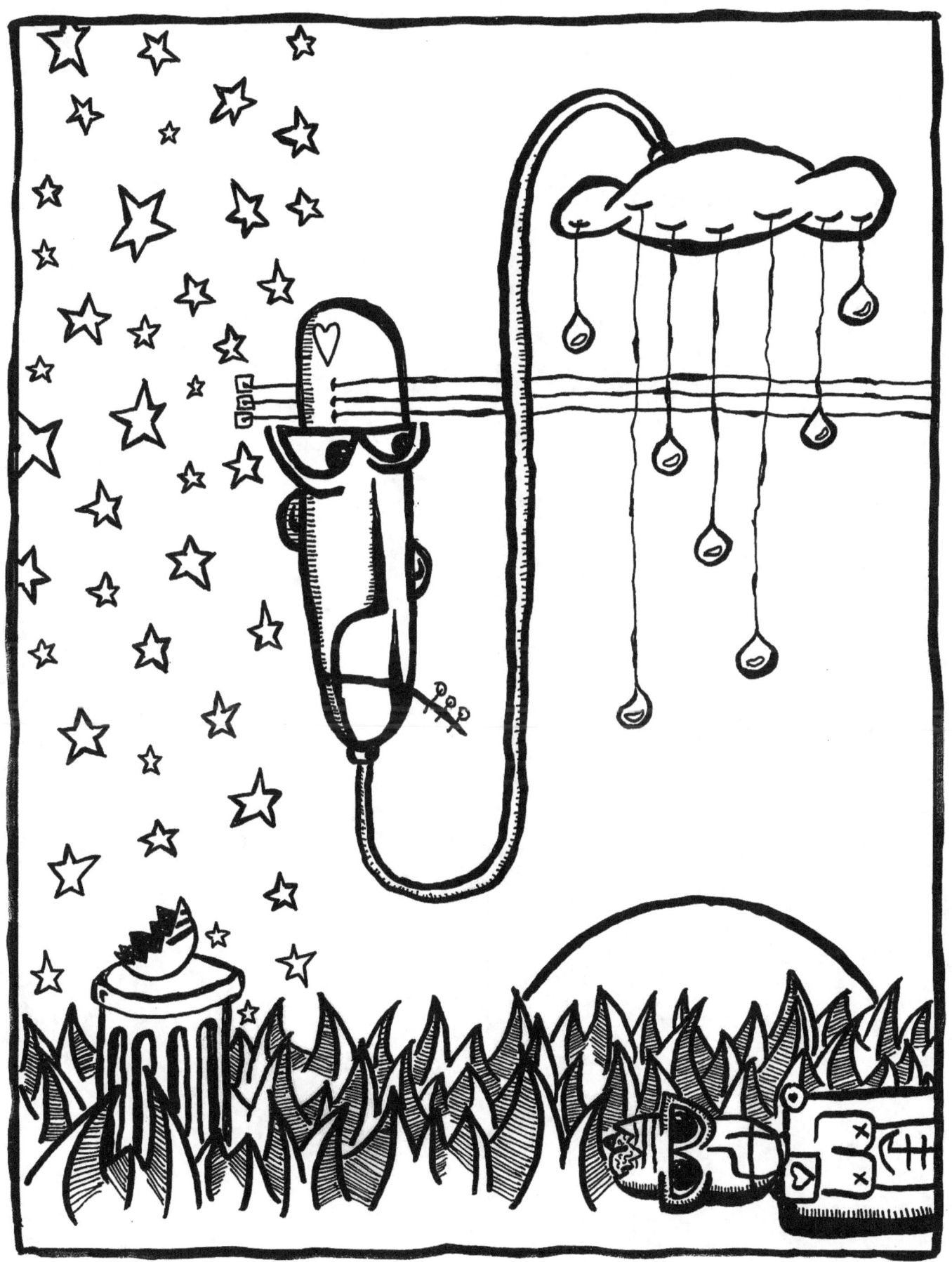

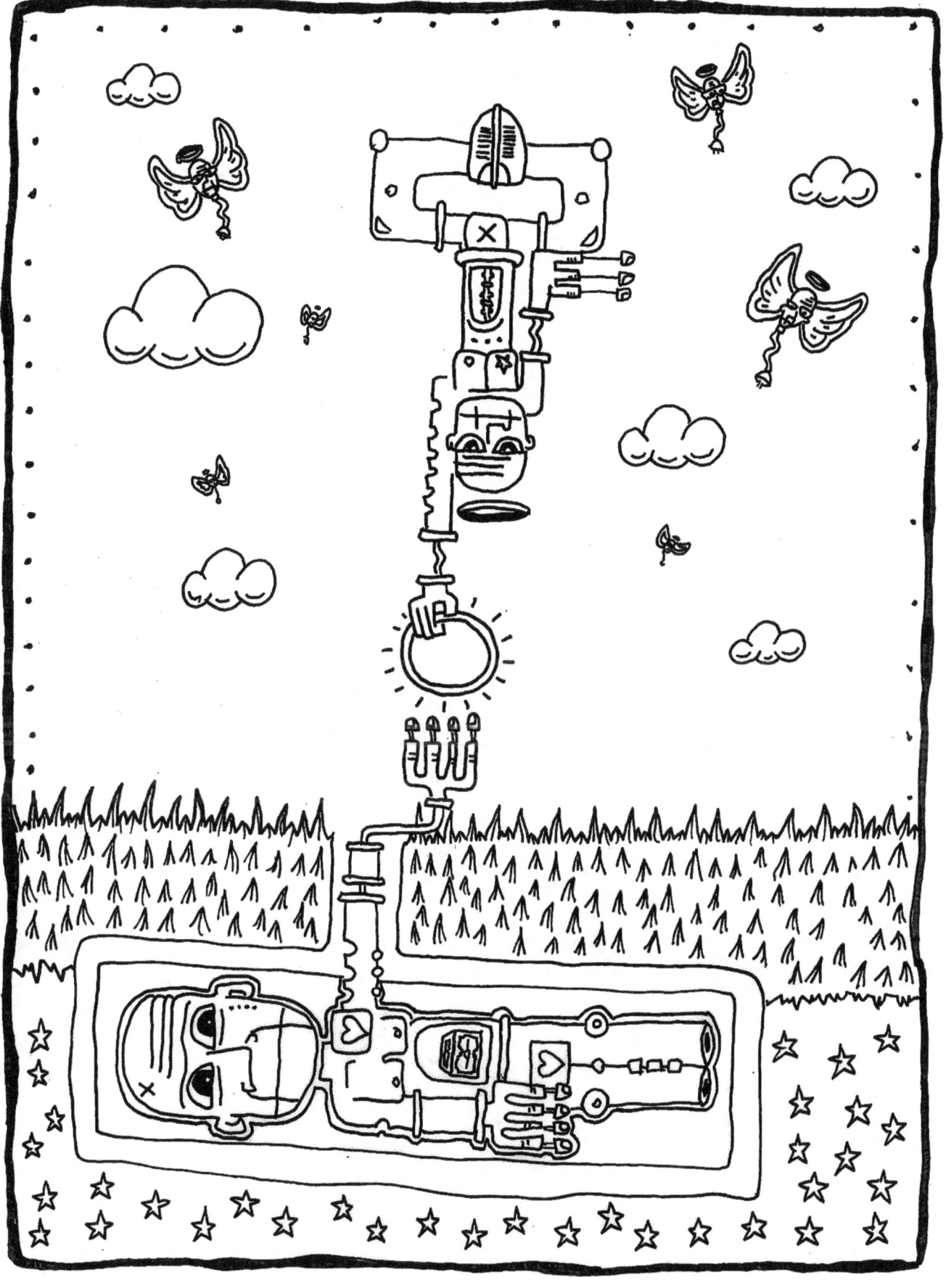

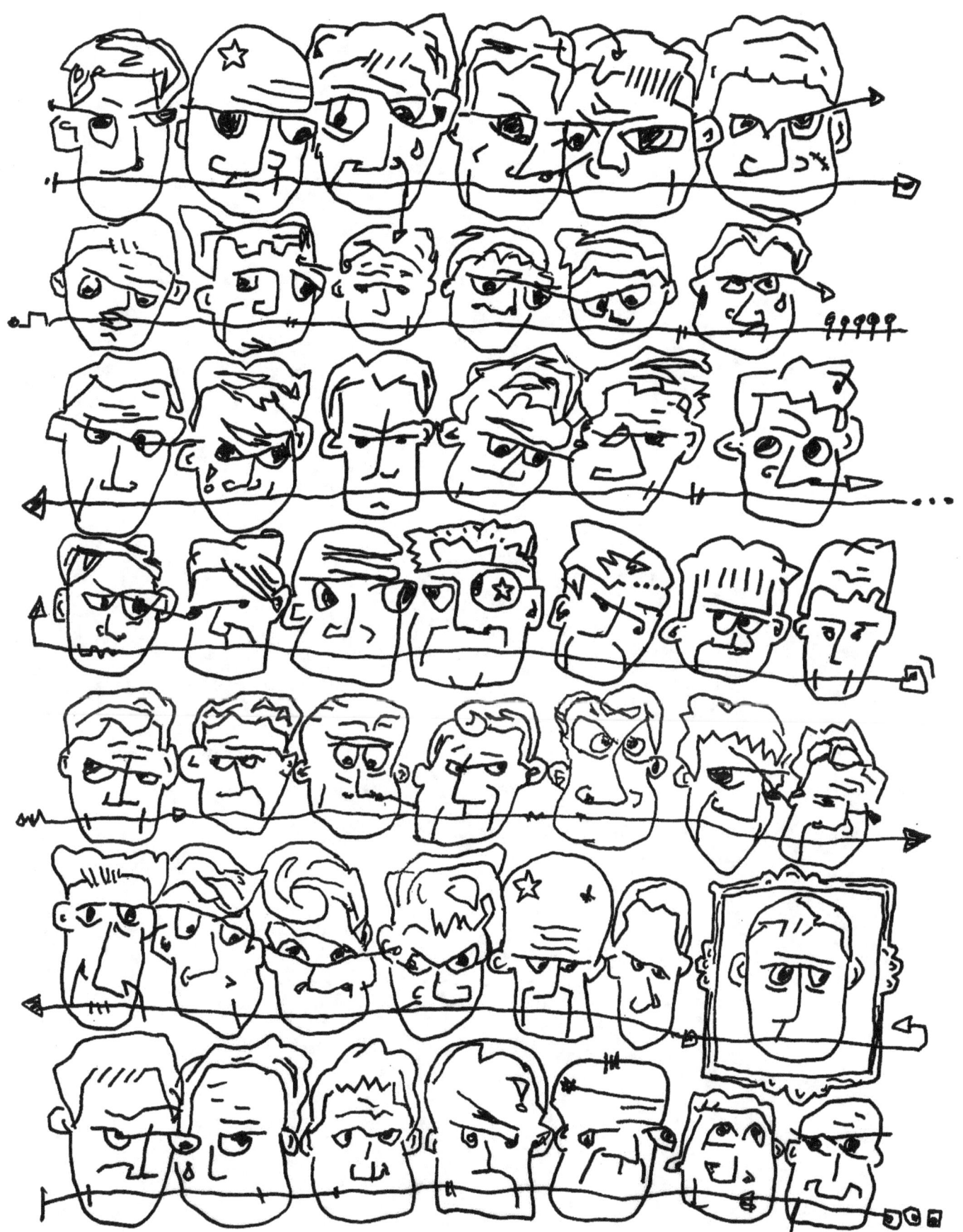

ABOUT THE ARTIST

Dan Drossman is a Brooklyn-based contemporary artist whose work encompasses fine art, guerilla street art, cartoon, and illustration. He holds an MFA from the School of Visual Arts, New York, and he and his work have been featured in publications such as *Studio Visit Magazine, NY Arts,* and *Art Forum,* and in venues such as David Zwirner Gallery, and the Open Air Museum in Sardenia, Italy. *Teetering The Line: An Adult Coloring Book* is his first book.